Yes We Kahn

By Joe Tracy and Kahn the Cat

ISBN-13: 978-0692283783

ISBN-10: 0692283781

If you would like to interview the author, please email Joe Tracy at joe@kahnthecat.com.

Follow Kahn the Cat
Website: www.KahnTheCat.com
Twitter: twitter.com/kahnthecat
YouTube: youtube.com/user/kahnthecat
Pinterest: pinterest.com/kahnthecat

Follow *Yes We Kahn*
Website: YesWeKahn.org
Pinterest: pinterest.com/yeswekahn

Yes We Kahn

Yes We Kahn is a book with a mission. The book was created in 10 days to help pay for unexpected emergency hospitalization for Kahn the Cat.

But it goes beyond that. Once all of Kahn's bills and care are covered, royalties will go to help families in similar situations through charities and contributions. You can track these donations at the book's Website, YesWeKahn.org.

Special Thanks for Saving Kahn's Life:
Dr. Courtney Smith
Dr. Katherine Scollan
Misha Thompson
Dr. Eddy Meese - "You Make It"

Additional Thanks
Mesheal Heyman for editing and for being Kahn's best friend.
"Grandma Joyce" for coming through for us and Kahn.
Our neighbors across the street who donated items for our yard sale to help raise funds for Kahn.
To **you** for buying this book, which helps Kahn and other cats/ pets in need of emergency assistance.

KAHN

Yes We Kahn

Thank you for taking this journey with me and for helping to give me a second chance at life through your purchase of this book.

Hopefully we can help other cats as well. The more fellow cats I can help, the more followers I'll have for my quest to rule the world...

My name is KAHN. My handlers wanted to name me after the great warrior Genghis Khan.

Do you see the problem?

I forgive them.
They are *human*, after all.

I'm really sick right now. But don't pity me. I'm strong, I'm courageous, I'm KAHN!

My destiny is yet to be fulfilled. And it starts with this book.

Here's a bit about me...

Let's start with "the look."

Growing up, my handlers were blessed with this look when they gave me something dumb to play with. Like this

DOG TOY

Would you tolerate such an injustice? I expect to have my own toys like...

BIRDS, GOOGLE GLASSES, IPAD

When not giving them "the look," here's how I *control* my handlers...

When I want their attention, I act cute!

When I have an itch, I meow. That gets me a scratch.

In short, I reward them when they do what I want.

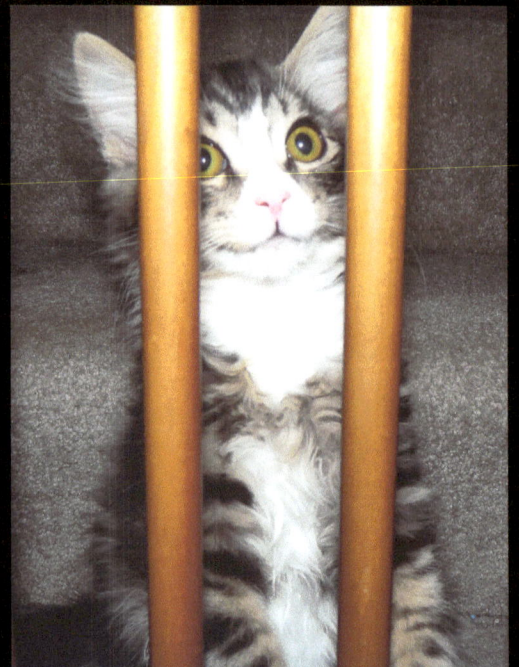

The point is that humans are *easy* to control. It's like that Pavlov dog experiment.

Every time you do what I want, I give you a reward.

"Fetch human! Good boy!"

I'm unique in many ways. I appear to have a very rare condition among cats called Portosystemic Shunt (known by humans as a Liver Shunt).

In short, my *warrior* blood travels around my liver instead of through it.

I've learned that these special conditions (or abilities) come with perks. I'm the only cat in the house my handlers let into the bedroom and office.

Then again, great leaders are always given special treatment.

Famous Quotes by Kahn:
"If you give a cat an inch, it will take a mile.
Therefore give the cat a mile to begin with."
- Kahn the Cat, 2011

My handlers adopted me from a shelter. It is called Salem Friends of Felines and is a place where humans try to get into the good graces of cats by finding us homes.

I was quick to find a home because every home needs a leader. How *lucky* my handlers were to be chosen by me!

I'm a very talented cat. Kahn Magazine named me the most eligible bachelor on the planet!

Leadership requires a plethora of training. I am well versed in the art of:

PLAYING DRUMS
LOOKING CUTE
WRESTLING WITH DOGS
ROARING (my handlers call it "squeaking")
SPARRING WITH DARTH VADER (a hero of mine)

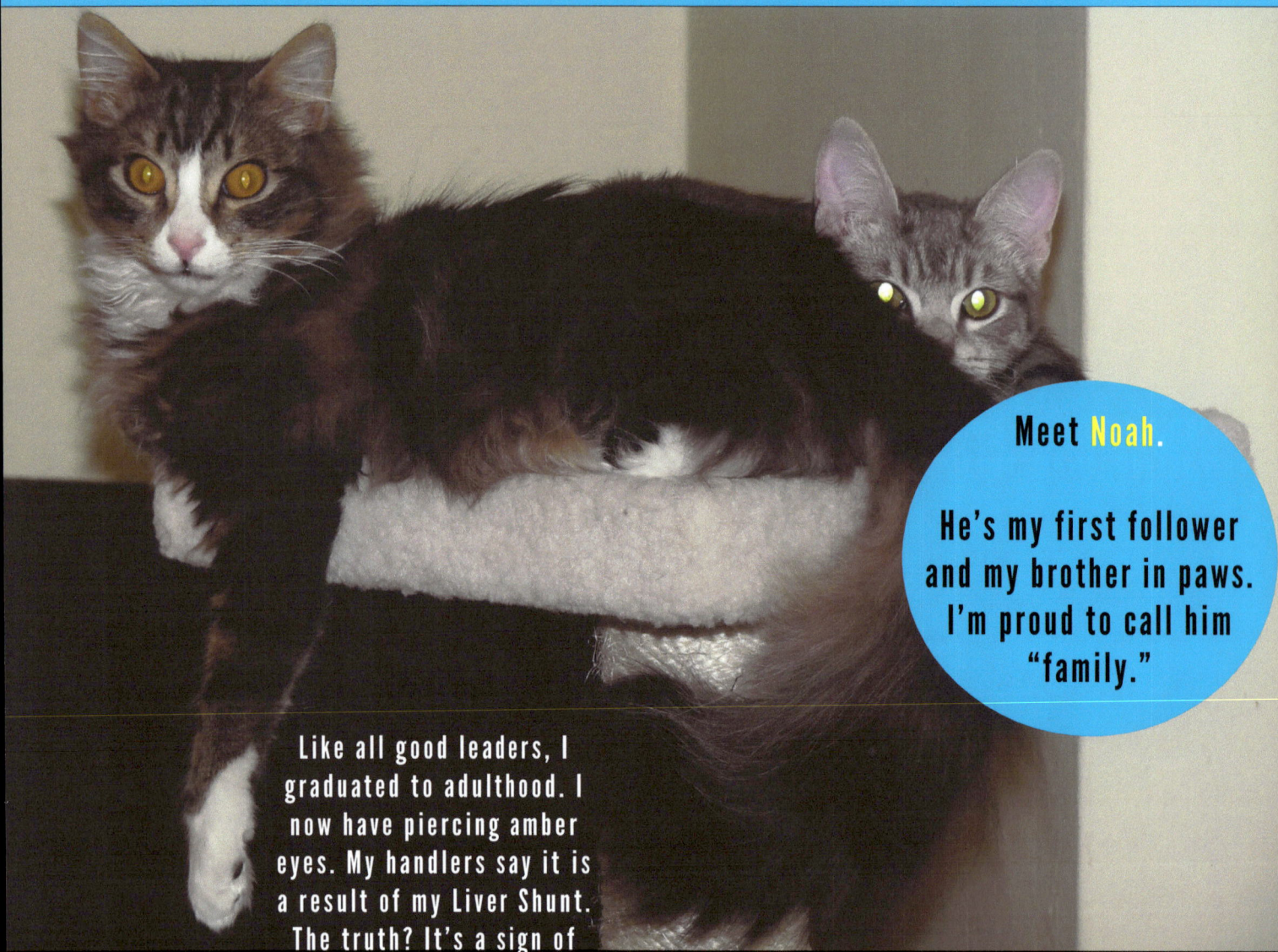

Meet Noah.

He's my first follower and my brother in paws. I'm proud to call him "family."

Like all good leaders, I graduated to adulthood. I now have piercing amber eyes. My handlers say it is a result of my Liver Shunt. The truth? It's a sign of me being the chosen one. I am Neo. I am James Bond. I am Darth Vader.
I AM KAHN!

Famous Quotes by Kahn:
"The paw is mightier than the sword."
- Kahn the Cat, 2013

Humans have a saying that goes, "If life hands you lemons, make lemonade."

My saying is: "If life hands you dry food, don't eat it. Meow until you get wet food."

Famous Quotes by Kahn:
"Early to bed and early to rise, makes a man healthy, wealthy, and wise. Therefore make sure your handler goes to bed late and doesn't get a good night's rest."

- Kahn the Cat, 2011

WE RUN

Scan the QR Code on the left (with your phone or tablet) to see my YouTube *Ninja Kitty* movie trailer video from 2010.

As a leader and warrior, I did ninja training as a kitten (see my *Ninja Kitty* video online).

That training has helped me to find some great hiding places. <-- What do you think?

Also important in ninja training is the ability to be flexible and contort your body like my picture to the right.

I'm young and I've trained well, but nothing prepared me for what happened on August 18, 2014...

During the morning I wasn't feeling good.

Something was wrong.

I remember having a lot of trouble breathing. And I was making this strange gurgling sound.

My handlers took me to that place I hate, where people in white coats poke at you. But this time I didn't seem to care. I was too tired.

When we got there I remember vomiting red stuff. My handlers cried.

After more examination, I heard them tell my handlers my lungs were full of fluid and my heart was really big (first time anyone's said I have a big heart - it was kind of touching).

But they said I might die.

I didn't mind. I just wanted the pain to end... *and that's the last I remember.*

The choice was euthanasia or try to drive Kahn an hour away to the vet hospital at Oregon State University.

The odds were high that he would die on the way, suffocating on the fluids in his lungs.

We wavered, deciding first to euthanize him so that he could die comfortably with family around him. But we changed our minds.

Kahn was rushed to the car. "You Make It," said the vet to Kahn.

Lois Bates Acheson Veterinary Teaching Hospital
Oregon State University

Kahn made it to the hospital, but he was in serious condition. For two days he was in ICU while doctors worked on stabilizing him and finding the cause.

The final prognosis was that Kahn had congestive heart failure. He has heart disease and it is estimated that he now has 4-12 months to live. One of Kahn's best household friends, a dog named Taco, died a year ago of congestive heart failure.

Sorry about that... It looks like my handlers hijacked my book. They like to do that with my blog, too!

I wasn't privy to all the doc to handler chat, but I will tell you that I have no plans of living within the confines of 4-12 months.

But even more important, please don't listen to the rumors that my best friend was a dog. It could ruin my sterling reputation.

There are several things I plan to accomplish before my permanent vacation in The Kingdom of Kahn (otherwise known as Kahndom).

> Get "Spandy Andy" to do a dance for me.
> Have a rap song written about me.
> Star in my own comic book.
> Be declared a national hero.
> Appear on a postage stamp.
> Catch the elusive laser dot.
> Take my handlers to the doctor's office for shots.

Scan the code above to get updates on Kahn's condition from KahnTheCat.com

Scan the code above to see the *Kahn Versus the World* movie trailer on YouTube

I have ambitions and aspirations. And since my near death experience, I have a "bucket list" too.

The key to achieving your goals and dreams is knowing how to get there. And as I always say: "Ask not what Kahn can do for you... Ask what you can do for Kahn."

I do look forward to one day leading the world. My largest (and most fun) aspiration will help me do that. And that would be...

Superhero Aspirations

Have you ever wondered why all superheroes portrayed in the movies are human?

Fear not! I am Kahn the Cat and I will use my brains and brawn to save you.

"Look! It's a bird! It's a plane! It's... A cat?"

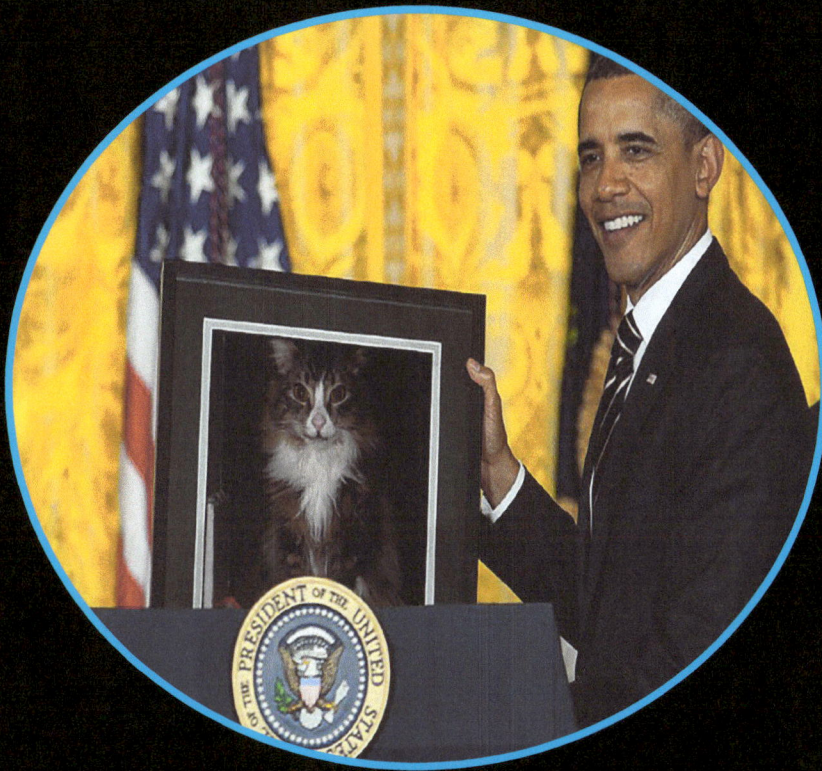

My platform for winning your vote to rule the world is simple:

> Free health care for cats!
> Funding for a hairball cure.
> Scratch posts for all cats.
> No dogs in the White House.
> Legalize catnip in all countries.
> Canned wet food for everyone.
> More cat videos on YouTube.
> Equality for all... cats.
> Free vacations on CATalina Island.
> Require employers to give all employees CATnaps four times daily.

Famous Quotes by Kahn:
"Give a man a fish and you feed him for a day. Give a man a cat and that cat will eat the fish for him."
- Kahn the Cat, 2014

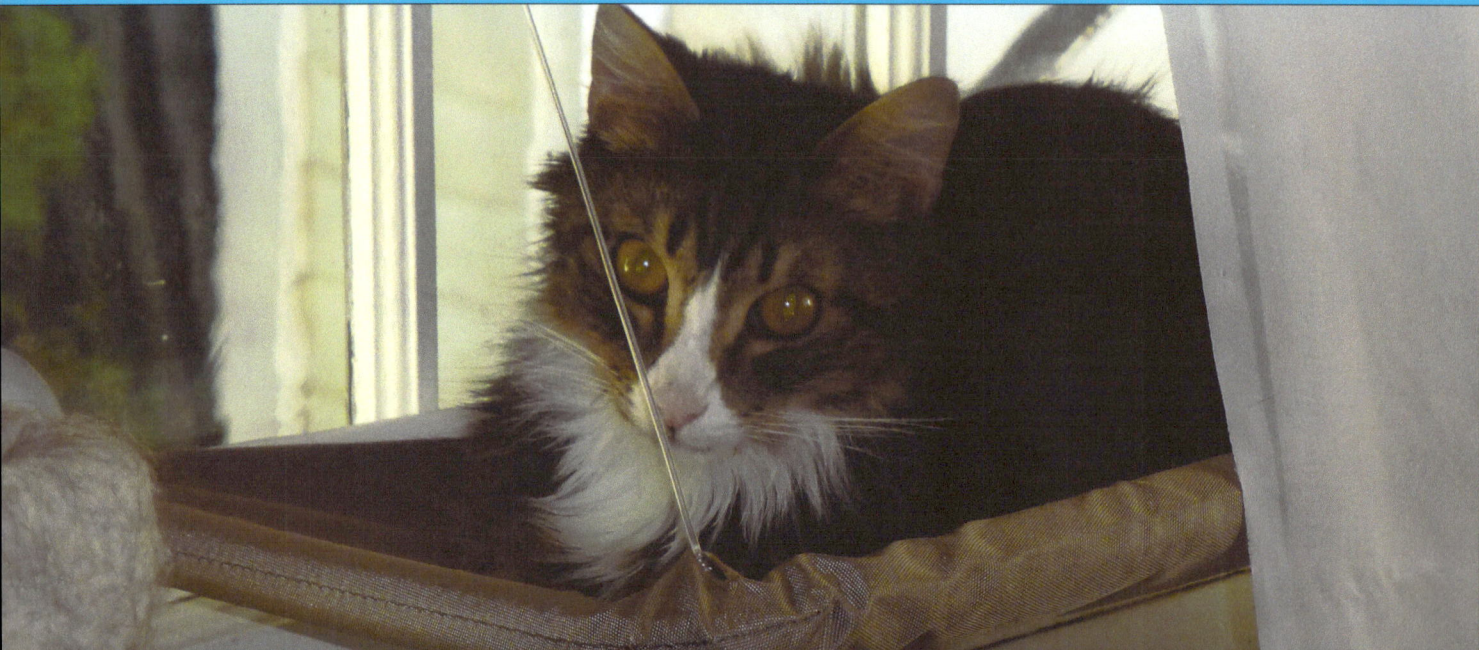

The above photo is the most
recent one taken of Kahn the Cat.

It was taken 10 days after his
hospitalization and the same day
his book, *Yes We Kahn* was completed.

Famous Quotes by Kahn:
"When the going gets tough, take a nap."
- Kahn the Cat, 2014

What You Can Do

If you enjoyed this book and its mission, then:
> Please review this book on Amazon.com.
> Please share the book link with your family/friends.
> Please mention the book on your Website if you have one.
> Please visit/bookmark KahnTheCat.com and YesWeKahn.org.
> Please find others you can help (see below).

If this book succeeds then we will be writing another book that outlines everything we did for the *Yes We Kahn* campaign so that other pet owners in emergency situations can find help in covering their emergency expenses.

You can find *Yes We Kahn* T-shirts and other products at Kahn's official Website - KahnTheCat.com.

If you want to find other cats/pets that you can help, then search GoFundMe.com and type in "cat" (or "dog") and peruse situations where you may be able to contribute. Also, do a search for organizations that help pet owners out in emergency situations.

THANK YOU! - joe@kahnthecat.com | kahn@kahnthecat.com

THANK YOU

www.ingramcontent.com/pod-product-compliance
Lightning Source LLC
LaVergne TN
LVHW072100070426
835508LV00002B/201

9780692283783